BRADFORD

Edited by Allison Dowse

First published in Great Britain in 1999 by
POETRY NOW YOUNG WRITERS
Remus House, Coltsfoot Drive,
Woodston,
Peterborough, PE2 9JX
Telephone (01733) 890066

HB ISBN 0 75431 506 1
SB ISBN 0 75431 507 X

FOREWORD

Poetry Now Young Writers have produced poetry books in conjunction with schools for over eight years; providing a platform for talented young people to shine. This year, the Celebration 2000 collection of regional anthologies were developed with the millennium in mind.

With the nation taking stock of how far we have come, and reflecting on what we want to achieve in the future, our anthologies give a vivid insight into the thoughts and experiences of the younger generation.

We were once again impressed with the quality and attention to detail of every entry received and hope you will enjoy the poems we have decided to feature in *Celebration 2000 Bradford* for many years to come.

CONTENTS

Swain House Middle School

Woodhouse Grove School

The Poems

A TIGER WHO WANTS TO BE FREE

I saw a tiger who wanted to be free
and that's because she wanted to catch me.
So I ran as fast as I could
but she got up in a bad tempered mood.
So I ran forward in a rush
but she was sitting there by the bush.
So I ran backward and sat next to the tree
but she was there, scratching at a flea.
But she didn't see what was near her
so she fell into the quarry.
Now small cubs must worry.

Lulu Begum (12)
Manningham Middle School

THE TIGER

He has . . .
Eyes as gold as amber
Claws as sharp as knives
Teeth as strong as fire
Fur as soft as velvet.

He needs . . .
Golden eyes - not blue
Sharp claws - not blunt
Strong teeth - not weak
Soft fur - not rough.

He wants . . .
To be free and have life
To have friends and not be lonely
To be a hunter on his own
To make people afraid of him.
That's the tiger!

Anne-Marie Nicholls (11)
Manningham Middle School

THE TIGER

He needs . . .
Eyes like lights in the dark
Claws like knives to cut his food
Fur so soft to cushion his fall.

He wants . . .
A safe home in the jungle
A big plump deer to eat
Some rainwater to quench his thirst
But most of all, he wants freedom and life.

He has . . .
Shoulders strong as iron bars
Limbs like wheels of a racing car
Teeth as sharp as stalactites
A brain as clever as a computer
And fur as warm as heaters
Then that's a description of a tiger!

Arfan Akhtar (11)
Manningham Middle School

AT A FIREWORK DISPLAY
(Inspired By 'Ping Pong' By Gareth Owen)

The crowd are anxious
The display men are patient
The fireworks are set to go off.
Waiting three, two, one . . .

Snap	Crackle
Fizz	Whizz
Pop	Roar
Zizzle	Sizzle

Bang!

Stop!	Fire away
Splunter	Sputter
Jerk	Querk
Squeak	Shimmer
Smack	Crack

Splat!

Stop!	Fire away
Buzz	Whir
Yap	Yowl
Shriek	Shrill
Blast	Crash

Wow-wee
Wow-wee
Wow-wee
Silence!

Baharun Nessa Ali (12)
Manningham Middle School

TIGER'S POEM

Tigers are not friendly
Tigers are not kindly
They don't act stupidly
They live happily.
When they see an animal they run
They don't want to live in cages - sadly
They want to live like other animals - freely
They just want to live normally.
They catch animals easily
They run quickly
As the wind blows fiercely
They look up in the sky and are lonely.
Tigers are kindly with their cubs
They handle them gently.
They catch small animals cruelly
but touch cubs softly.

Halima Bibi (12)
Manningham Middle School

TIGER, TIGER BURNING BRIGHT

Tiger, tiger burning bright
you do have such fiery eyes
looking at the peaceful night
your claws are sharp as knives.

Tiger, tiger burning bright
you'd rather be fierce than timid.
Tiger, your patterns are vivid
you snarl in your cage
you're too old for your age.

Tiger, tiger burning bright
you are strong, with all your might.
Grasping anything in your way
and searching your perfect prey.

Tiger, tiger burning bright
protecting cubs in the night.
Doing things that seem just right
keeping eyes on all in sight.

Tiger, tiger burning bright
you do have such fiery eyes
looking at the peaceful night
your claws are sharp as knives.

Shafia Begum (11)
Manningham Middle School

TIGER

At the bottom of the beautiful thick tall trees
in the forest rests
an unfriendly, frightening tiger.
He wants to be fierce, not friendly,
he wants to be fast not slow,
he wants to be free not locked up in the zoo.

He needs . . .
Eyes that sparkle like fire,
Whiskers that feel like silk,
Claws that shine like crystal,
Ears which are soft as cotton,
Fur that feels like velvet,
Limbs that are strong and fit,
And a body that's strong and feels like wool.

He has claws to lash,
He has colourful fur,
Teeth as white as snow,
Big round eyes which glow.

S M Rejwan Malik (12)
Manningham Middle School

A TIGER'S LIFE

It lies camouflaged in long thick grass
It runs as fast as a truck
It stares as plump deer run by
It's ready to hunt down its prey.

It lies camouflaged in long thick grass
Through the jungle it protects
its cubs from any foes.
Keeping them out of danger.

It lies camouflaged in long thick grass
Its claws are like sharp stinging spikes.
Its eyes are like shiny gold
Its fur is soft as velvet.

It lies camouflaged in long thick grass
It's bloodthirsty like a vampire.
It rips animals apart like a mad creature
Its prey's blood drips from its teeth.

Imran Ali (11)
Manningham Middle School

TIGER

Eyes as bright as the light
a supple body
claws that are clutching tight
and a cunning smile.

His gleaming eyes in the night
glowing in the dark.
He glances around himself
greedily looking for prey.

His powerful paws
as strong as metal
and his jaws open wide
to swallow down prey.

A sparkle in his eye
shining in the dark.
Gently laying down
falling sound asleep.

Aishah Kauser (12)
Manningham Middle School

THE CHASE

Zoom down the stairs
Dash for the front door
Frantically struggle with the handle
See a shadowy figure
A knife
No! A dagger
Heavy thudding footsteps approaching
Come closer and closer

Mohammed Abdul Wazed (11)
Manningham Middle School

COLOUR POEM

Sitting near the brightening fire
flames are firing.
The sun is shining, time to have some
delicious custard.
Pleasant and sweet, ready to eat
with some lemon pie.

Majid Rashid (11)
Manningham Middle School

WAR

Football is a war
People chasing each other
Throwing each other on the floor
In the end one is always
Victorious!

Mohammed Ali (12)
Manningham Middle School

BLACK

A sneaky spider slowly crawls past me
coldness fills the whole room
as I stare into nothing but darkness.
For it seems like night is here forever.

Yasmin Ali (12)
Manningham Middle School

AUTUMN

As I open the front door
a whiff of cold air hits my face.
I freeze in the doorway
dreading that I have to walk out.
I let myself out of the door
knowing my warm clothes will protect me.
Crunch, crunch the leaves go
as I stomp my way to school.
Drops of rain start drizzling down,
the wind starts howling at me
and leaves are flying all around.
The twigs are crackling at my feet
then everything goes quiet
I found myself at the entrance of my school.

Sabiah Farooq (12)
Manningham Middle School

A PACK OF LIES

(Inspired By 'I Saw A Peacock With A Fiery Tail' Anon)

I saw a mouse save the king
I saw a hero dance and sing.
I saw a musician lay its eggs.
I saw a bird hunt for a peg.
I saw a pupil waggle its tail.
I saw a dog scream and wail.
I saw a baby jump in the pool.
I saw a frog sitting on a stool.
I saw a man in a cocoon.
I saw a caterpillar late at noon.
I saw a cat erode the rocks.
I saw a river with a thousand locks.
I saw a door limping by.
I saw an old man baking a pie.
I wrote this poem and that's not a lie.

Zahra Saleem (11)
Manningham Middle School

A SAD STORY

When I was four in Pakistan,
I always wanted a pet lamb.
One day my wish came true,
my mother came home with a few.
Mine was the little one around the corner,
with a sweet smile, I named him Smiler.

We had . . .

happy times	quiet times
sad times	lonely times
noisy times	jolly times

But I never knew there had to be *death times!*

Look after your pet
Don't give it too much to eat
or else it might die!

Salma Parveen (11)
Manningham Middle School

MY CRUEL TEACHER

My teacher is a cruel witch
her overgrown nose sticks out
two metres away.
She marks my work with her
revolting, wrinkled hands.
She keeps me in her cage
which she calls a classroom.
She drinks children's blood
though she calls it tomato juice.
She flies home on a broom
and comes to school in an
old fashioned car.
I call her Ms Brown.

Sobia Asghar (12)
Manningham Middle School

BLACK

... as the devil
... as evil
... as a nightmare
... as dead blood
on a grey neck.
The vampire has sucked!

Mahbub Ali (11)
Manningham Middle School

WINTER IS A KNIFE

Winter is a knife
deadly and hazardous
cutting winds stab my face.
Winter is something you're
not supposed to mess with.
If you do
you're skating on thin ice.

Ashraf Ali (11)
Manningham Middle School

AUTUMN

My sister is autumn
the leaves are her spots.
The rain comes slushing down her nose,
her eyes half drooping down.
Not so much sunlight.
Her snore is thunder
her scream is lightning.
She fades away slowly
as winter approaches through the door
I say 'Hi Dad!'

Shazia Aziz (11)
Manningham Middle School

HIGH ON THE HILL

Up on the top of the highest hill
above the dewy emerald fields,
glistening in the sun.
Above the spurting river
gushing down to the sea
above the quivering aspen and spruce trees.
Where lie the nests of pigeons and crows
above the fluttering insects
always hovering about.

Aisha Ditta (12)
Manningham Middle School

STUPIDITY

I saw a chair galloping by
I saw a horse wearing a tie
I saw a man chasing his tail
I saw a dog open the mail
I saw my neighbour crawl up the wall
I saw my spider slide through a hole
I saw my snake cook my bread
I saw my baker with a plastic head
I saw my doll tied with a guy
I saw a chair galloping by.

Abeer Kaiser (12)
Manningham Middle School

BLACK

As the blackberry buds close
in the pitch dark, strangers are walking
as the danger's about.
The sun comes up and people are talking
as the moon fades away
the sun gives a ray.
As the birds are singing
the bells are ringing.

Rahel Choudhury (12)
Manningham Middle School

YELLOW

The sun shines like a dazzling ball
I look out from the window
I see the sunflowers come out
Children playing merrily
as they skip in the meadow.
I look at the stony sand
and the water coming towards
the shore.

Shamima Hashim (12)
Manningham Middle School

WHITE

The moon shining in the night
a light of a lamp.
A plain shirt and a lovely wedding dress
inside an open wardrobe.
Two half-filled milk glasses and
two silver tins, one for sugar
the other for salt.
On the floor a small crunched-up paper
Written on it was goodnight!

Azima Ali (12)
Manningham Middle School

MOUSE

I have a mouse
so quiet and creepy.
He steals things from my room
he hides away from me when
we are asleep in the night.
He tiptoes around the house
I call him my little brother.

Ibrahim Ali (11)
Manningham Middle School

A CRUEL EYE

He dashed down the stairs
his hand trembled with fear
as he struggled with the handle.
There wasn't a sound of anybody.
He banged open the letter box
Screamed for help . . .
A shadow of a black dagger appeared.

Sultana Khatun (11)
Manningham Middle School

GREEN

Grasshoppers are hopping,
The wind is blowing,
Trees are swishing,
dropping green ripe apples.
Frogs are resting on lilypads
burping loudly and unpleasantly.
Green leaves are falling,
Brown leaves are appearing,
Summer has disappeared
while autumn has appeared.

Asif Rosaf (12)
Manningham Middle School

WATCHING

I sat at the top
of the tallest tree.

Watching the animals
that are free.

Watching me sitting
up there, with eyes
full of hatred.

Watching, watching me
as if they want me for tea.

Watching them
I might
stumble down
get beaten
then eaten.

Anisa Khousar (12)
Manningham Middle School

MY DOG

My dog is called Lance
in dog years he's older than me
he's even over thirty three!

I have a Dwarfe rabbit he's only six
he's fond of chewing on sticks.
His back is white his patches are black
his biggest patch is on his back.

I had some fish but they died
and only one of them survived.
She lives in my pond all by herself
I have a picture of her on my shelf.

I wish I had more dogs
also in my pond are frogs.

Georgina Lennon (9)
St Francis RC Primary School, Eccleshill

SPACE

Ever quiet and peaceful
ever noiseless and still.
The outer reaches of space
undisturbed.
It will stay like that until
selfish humans invade the
tranquillity.
Invade, conquer, kill
every lifeform crushed to dust
and humans rule the Universe.
Civilisations burnt to rubble
never to be rebuilt.

The calm and peace now filled with
noise.
Humans should be content, but
still yearn for more.
Ever conquering
Ever capturing
When will they ever learn that
the Universe is a wonderful place
to be shared with one and all.

Patrick Friis (11)
St Francis RC Primary School, Eccleshill

WHAT IS . . .

What is cool? The breeze is cool
making me feel at ease.

What is hot? The cooker is hot
cooking my tea for me
and when it's nearly done
I look in 'Oh, it's done!'
So now I'm all fat and plump.

What is sleep? Dreams are sleep
dreaming me away to dreamland.
I may peep into fairyland.
No one knows!

Ashleigh Walker (9)
St Francis RC Primary School, Eccleshill

DIFFERENT COLOURS

What is red, orange and green?
The traffic lights are red, orange and green
they tell you when to stop, get ready and go.

What is yellow? Leaves are sometimes yellow
when they're falling off tall trees.

What is pink? Pigs are pink up in a farm
on a hill.

What is green? Grasshoppers are green
hopping about the garden grass.

What is purple? Grapes are purple,
juicy and nice.

What is blue? The sea is blue
fish swimming about all over.

Jade Deering Holmes (11)
St Francis RC Primary School, Eccleshill

MY BEST FRIEND

My best friend likes playing games
she has more friends than I do.
I think her cat is so cute
but my cat is dead.
So God please look after him.

Emma Rose Wilkinson (7)
St Francis RC Primary School, Eccleshill

THE MAN

His nickname is the man
His real name is Stan.
He hit my best friend with a frying pan.
He is really cool.
He can swim five lengths of the pool.
He is really bad
Some people say he's mad.
He is very strong,
He can even beat up King Kong!
He lives in a giant house,
He squashed a tiny mouse.
He owns a massive angry dog,
Which killed and ate
A cat called Mog.

Nick Albrow (9)
St Francis RC Primary School, Eccleshill

SHOOTING STAR

One afternoon I went outside
there was something glowing
I was so surprised.

It was amazing, it was fantastic
was it just a piece of elastic?
Then it faded out of sight
I said to myself 'Should I come out tonight?'
Maybe so, maybe not
is my sister still in her cot?
I went outside on that night
and then I saw a glimmer of light
just coming into sight on that night.

Rachael Atkinson (8)
St Francis RC Primary School, Eccleshill

My Cat

My cat is called Snap
she is ginger and white
she has a red collar
green eyes and a pink nose.
She is three and once she got stung
by a bumble bee.

Since I moved house
my cat ran away.
I think about her
every single day.

Georgia Narey (9)
St Francis RC Primary School, Eccleshill

AUTUMN

As the summer's gone
and the winter's coming,
I know what time of year it is,
it's autumn.

When the leaves turn brown
and they start to fall
I know what time of year it is,
it's autumn.

When my friends are inside
I go out to play.
I know what time of year it is
it's autumn.

Before Christmas
after the holidays
I know what time of year it is
it's autumn.

Nicola Wetherell (9)
St Francis RC Primary School, Eccleshill

I LIKE PEOPLE

I like people
I love me
I love the seaside
I love the sea.

I like people
I love me
I love sausage rolls
I love tea.

I love people
I love me
I love my dogs
I have three.

Jack Scully (8)
St Francis RC Primary School, Eccleshill

MY PETS

In my house
I have a Bulldog that's thick
and a large chubby pig.
I have a dark black cat
and a little funny bunny.
I have two tiny hamsters
that climb on their cage.
Next there's a mouse
that sometimes runs away.
There are two donkeys
that make noises in the night.
Oh, and I can't forget the
16 spiders, they spin webs on
my bed.
My brother doesn't like these pets
so tough luck - they're staying!

Matthew Smith (8)
St Francis RC Primary School, Eccleshill

SORRY MISS!

Sorry for snapping the ruler Miss,
Sorry for throwing the pen
Sorry for disturbing Lindsay Miss
From counting to one hundred and ten.

Sorry for sketching on the rubber Miss,
Sorry for starting to talk.
Sorry for putting the bin on Carl's head
Miss - sorry for snapping the chalk.

Sorry for hitting Laura Miss,
Sorry for banging the door.
Sorry for tearing the page in that book
I won't do it anymore.

Sorry for copying Amy's work Miss,
When I should have been doing my own.
I bet you're fed up with me now Miss,
I guess I should go home.

Natalie Firth (9)
St Francis RC Primary School, Eccleshill

WHAT IS . . .

What is green? Seaweed is green
all slimy but clean.

What is blue? The sea is blue
it grew and grew.

What is orange? The sunset is orange
when the summer's due.

What is yellow? Honey is yellow
ready for the bumble bees.

What is purple? Pansies are purple
making friends with the turtle.

What is pink? Roses are pink
by the garden's brink.

Beatrice Brown (10)
St Francis RC Primary School, Eccleshill

HOW YOU FEEL WHEN YOU ARE WRITING A POEM

Tears
pain
empty brain
unhappy
sad
nasty
untame
crazy
cheeky
weird
hate it
mean
not clever
awful!

Emily Dobbie (9)
St Francis RC Primary School, Eccleshill

WEATHER

I stood outside I wished I was dry
the rain came down from the dark misty sky.
I shook and waggled just like our boxer dog
I went inside.
The wind was howling and growling
the wind was as bad as before.
I love it when it's snowy
I love it when it rains.
But the one thing I just can't stand is
when the thunder gives me pains.

Laura Sheerin (9)
St Francis RC Primary School, Eccleshill

PENCILS

Pencils are great,
You can draw with them,
Scribble,
Whack with them,
Flick them,
Snap them,
Colour with them,
Mess about with them
But the one thing I hate about pencils
Is working with them!

Christopher Doonan (8)
St Francis RC Primary School, Eccleshill

THE MARMALADE KITTEN

The marmalade kitten
With stripes on his tail
Went down to the pond
When the wind blew a gale.

He stepped on a log,
But the wind was so strong
When he lifted his tail
It just blew him along
        Weeee!

Charlotte Heap (10)
St Francis RC Primary School, Eccleshill

EVERYTHING IS YUM YUM!

Everything is yum, yum,
I like cream buns.

Cream buns in a pot,
Out pops chocolate mmm, so hot.

Chocolate cake in my chops,
Out pops crisps and pop.

Crisps and pop on my knee,
Now I'm waiting for my tea!

Chloe Lockwood (10)
St Francis RC Primary School, Eccleshill

SORRY MUM

Sorry Mum for breaking the computer,
Sorry for kicking the TV.
Sorry Mum for smashing the window,
I'm very sorry as you can see.

Sorry for thumping my brother, Mum,
Sorry for smashing the ornament.
Sorry for moving the bricks, Mum,
With the wet cement.

Sorry for snapping the chair, Mum,
Sorry for ripping your letter.
Sorry for throwing milk on the video machine,
Please forgive me.

Lindsay Parnham (9)
St Francis RC Primary School, Eccleshill

MY FAMILY

Smelly socks on the floor,
Muddy boots jam the door.
Reading books on the bed,
Sticky glue on Godzilla's head,
        That's Carl.

Homework books on the floor,
Billie posters on the door.
Reading books on the shelf,
Crisps eaten by myself,
        That's me.

Dog poo on the floor,
He even weed by the door.
Dreaming of chicken legs,
He likes to scratch his furry head,
        That's Toto.

Claire Saunders (8)
St Francis RC Primary School, Eccleshill

MY PETS

Going to the toilet all over the kitchen floor
When you give her cat food
She always asks for more
       That's Max.

Kissing you when she's hungry
Climbs up the door
Sleeping on your head
Jumps on my brother's bed
       That's Lucky.

Running in her wheel
Sleeping up ahead
About one year old
And is nice and soft to hold
       That's Jody.

Megan Lianne Oldfield (9)
St Francis RC Primary School, Eccleshill

MY FAMILY

My dad is a softy
My mum is bossy
My gran lets me stay up late
My grandad shouts all the time
And my uncle, we don't like him.

Sam Riley (8)
St Francis RC Primary School, Eccleshill

MY FAMILY

My mum is bossy
My granny is rich
My sister is a witch
My dad works on a computer
My dog is a bitch (lady dog)
My favourite food is chocolate
And that is it!

Rebecca Brown (8)
St Francis RC Primary School, Eccleshill

MY BIG BROTHER

My big brother,
he's always mean to me
and when I first saw him,
I thought he looked like me.

I'm nasty to him,
he's nasty to me,
but when I'm kind to him,
he's always kind to me.

My brother's bigger than me,
but I don't care,
because I can still beat him,
so there!

Alex Bottomley (8)
St Francis RC Primary School, Eccleshill

My Family Poem

Underpants on the bed
Stickers on the window,
Leaves mucky clothes on the chair
That is Richard!

Clothes in the drawers
Teddies on the shelves
Homework on the desk
That is me.

Wool in the car
Golf things in the hall
Ties on the bannister
That is Dad.

Rachael Tempest-Mitchell (8)
St Francis RC Primary School, Eccleshill

IN THE GARDEN

In the garden I walk about
Smelling flowers on the ground.

I walk and play all around
'Urgh' what is that on the ground?

'Urgh' it's a spider on the leaves.

'Urgh' I won't pick it up
I'll get a disease.

Laura Pierce (9)
St Francis RC Primary School, Eccleshill

PET DESCRIPTIONS

Tess is giddy and loveable
Fish are boring
Goldie is sleepy and daft
Tess is furry and slobbery
Fish are slimy
Goldie is cute and cuddly
Tess is full of energy
Fish are bubbly
Goldie is furry and silly.

Gemma Fisher (8)
St Francis RC Primary School, Eccleshill

BIG SISTERS

My big sister is such a pain
She is enough to send you totally insane.
She has her music on every night
I just wish she was out of sight.
When she's out with her mates
And acting dead tough
I get a quick chance
To look in all of her private stuff.

She is hours in the bathroom
She never lets me in.
I'm hopping from one foot to another
Shouting 'Come on you ugly thing.'
She gets a bath every night
As late as can be.
If you go in there after her
You've got to be braver than *me!*

Amy Loxam (8)
St Francis RC Primary School, Eccleshill

SPRING IS COMING

Spring is coming,
Bees are buzzing,
Flowers are forming,
Dogs are snoring.

      Spring is coming,
      Rivers are running,
      Horses are trotting,
      Snow is rotting.

Spring is coming,
Birds are humming,
Sun is setting,
Men are betting.

          Spring is coming.

Faye Collins (11)
St Francis RC Primary School, Eccleshill

WHAT IS . . .

What is yellow, a banana is yellow,
What is pink, a crayon is pink,
What is red, a rose is red,
What is brown, a brick is brown,
What is orange, of course an orange is orange,
What is green, a piece of grass is green,
What is blue, a blueberry is blue,
What is black, the night sky is black,
What is white, the moon is white.

Kimberley Malloy (10)
St Francis RC Primary School, Eccleshill

THINKING POEM

I am writing this poem,
but I don't know what about,
looking in the dictionary,
looking at all these words
what shall I do it about?

I am thinking about this poem,
thinking what to write,
nothing in a dictionary,
nothing to do at all,
just what shall I do it about?

Well I've nothing to do,
just nothing to do at all,
although I could finish this poem,
so thank you for reading this poem,
so I'll say bye for now.

Sarah L Fox (10)
St Francis RC Primary School, Eccleshill

MY PETS!

My pets are really wacky,
My rats are really yacky.
My hamsters are really cutey,
My pythons are really ugly.
My Rottweilers are really vicious,
But my pigs are delicious.
My mice eat cheesy Cheetoes,
My kittens are really thin.

Martin Favell (9)
St Francis RC Primary School, Eccleshill

PET POEM

Ten donkeys in my bed,
Nine snakes in my underwear drawer.
Eight worms on my light,
Seven cats in my wardrobe.
Six boogie wigs in my drawer,
Five dead mice in my shoes.
Four fat rats in my pocket,
Three dinosaurs in my kitchen.
Two bears in my bath
And one of . . . guess who?

Ryan Newton (8)
St Francis RC Primary School, Eccleshill

MY SISTER IS ANNOYING

My sister is annoying
  she says I have:

  spotty trousers
    purple nose
      orange hair
        sandles
          baggy socks
            and a red face.

I get her back I say she is fat
  little
    and the slimiest girl in the
    world.
      She goes crying to Mum.

Myles Nesbitt (8)
St Francis RC Primary School, Eccleshill

CARTOONS

Looney Toons are cartoons,
Daffy's always in the cafe,
Bugs Bunny is so funny,
Elmer is always shooting Bugs Bunny
But Bugs is too funny.
Tazmania is always rushing around
And pushing folk around.
Dexter has to work something out himself,
Road Runner is very fast and he's even faster
Than a motorbike.
He's cool and you'll have to be fast to catch him.
Elmer's always got something to say
When he catches Bugs Bunny
Maybe it's this -
'Now what shall I do with you
Shall I shoot you?'
But Bugs always gets away.
>   *That's all folks.*

Joseph Hughes (9)
St Francis RC Primary School, Eccleshill

ANIMALS

Animals are cute
Alsatians are playful and exciting
Animals are furry and fluffy
Goldfish are slimy and boring
Snakes are horrible and hissy
Kittens are cute and fluffy
Fish are bubbly.

Alexandra Bolland (8)
St Francis RC Primary School, Eccleshill

PETS

I love to have a pet in the house,
A large Rottweiler or even a mouse.

It's amusing to have a pet in the house,
It's company if everyone's out.
If you buy a large dog
It's good to withhold robbers.

Michael O'Farrell (8)
St Francis RC Primary School, Eccleshill

A SHARK

A shark is mean
a shark is keen
but is also a bit deadly.

A shark is strange
a shark is long
but also feeds on us.

A shark eats guts
a shark eat liver
and it's going to eat you!

Carl McBride (7)
St Francis RC Primary School, Eccleshill

AMAZING ALLITERATION

An almond almost admitted his ambition to be an astronaut.
Barry the bouncer bounced brilliantly to Bermuda.
Cerry Cantona courteously created candles in Canada.
Dopey Darren died designing Donkey Disaster in Denmark.
Eight enormous elephants entertained Eskimos.
Fifty fat fish finished frying frogs on Friday.
Gigantic Jack jogged joyfully to Germany.
Hairy Helen hated hippopotamuses hiring historians.
India incredibly identified Indian Impalas.
Jumping John jumped to Jamaica drinking juice.
King Kong crammed corn into cones.
Lilly Lee logically lost the lottery.
Manpreet the mango marvellously, magically disappeared to mainland.
Naughty Norman nervously navigated nine nails to Netherlands.
Only olives and opticians over-ate oranges.
Penelope Piper progressively programmed problems.
Quentin Tarantino quit carrying carry bags.
Rushing rhinos remembered running reckless.
Silly Sam the snake slithered slowly, silently to Spain.
Thomas the Tank Engine took two tigers and tickled them.
Untidy umbrellas unwanted uplifting unicorns.
Vacuumed vans varied from vermilion and violet.
Whales washed windows while watching world's wonders.
Yummy yoghurt used yo-yos to York.
Zapping Zack zapped zebras, zombies and zoos.

Navraj Singh Riyait (10)
Swain House Middle School

SUMMER GARDEN

As the sun rises,
A beautiful butterfly flutters down like an
Autumn leaf in the wind.
Landing on a rose,
In the summer garden.

The drops of rain glisten on the roses,
In the slight breeze.
Bees whiz by,
Quickly trying to get to sparkling foxgloves.

Dragonfly and ladybird,
Dancing together on a gleaming pansy,
By the fence,
Two cats play happily with a sweet smelling leaf.

Small rabbits and hedgehogs,
Teasing spiders that run by,
Trying to find flies in their twinkling webs.

Now you know,
There is a lot more life,
In a summer garden!

Lisa Allen (11)
Swain House Middle School

ASTOUNDING ALLITERATION

One wicked witch waddled down a water melon
Two twilight twins twirl twice
Three thorns thrash thimbles
Four phenomenal fairies fiddled with fear
Five friendly fireflies focus on fluffy foam
Six silly sickly skittles skidded
Seven senseless sausages separate from sight
Eight elephants elegantly electrify
Nine nightingales nibble nice noodles
Ten technical teens tremble
Eleven elves elegantly electrify
Twelve twigs twiddled.

Chloe Walker (11)
Swain House Middle School

DEWDROPS

As the twinkling dew falls,
Upon the spring flowers,
Light sunshine falling,
The sea gleaming,
In view of the stars,
The rivers sparkle with light.

The sand,
Wet on the seashore.
The dripping sleet,
Falling on the frozen ground.
The trees bare,
Stood alone.

The days,
With drips of sunshine.
The nights,
With rippling moons.
Both day or night,
Both falling on the dunes.

Rachel Fisher (11)
Swain House Middle School

NUMBER TESTS

Times and divide,
With the multiplication,
If I don't get this question right
I am going to die.

That's too hard, that's nearly impossible,
Remember radius squared and times by pi.
A quadrilateral is a square,
And a rhombus is one pushed over.

This one is so easy,
I could do it in two minutes flat.
Wow, that sum is very vast,
Don't forget the zero on the end!

That is a sequence,
In triangular numbers up it goes in
One to five and five to one
Is the co-ordination of the very last one.

That was really hard,
But I'm glad it's done.
Now I've got the mental and the level six,
And I'm going to faint in shock!

Richard Magennis (10)
Swain House Middle School

MILLENNIUM

The millennium 2000 is just around the corner,
Will life change or just stay the same?
Will computers crash or just blow up?
I have dreams of aliens taking over the planet.
My excitement is building up inside me.

I want to look into the future in my magic crystal ball.
Will I wake up and be an alien monster?
I want to go to the Millennium Dome, but will it be ready or not?
Will I still be happy in the year 2000?
It all depends on what we call the millennium, the year 2000.

Samantha Hurd (11)
Swain House Middle School

MY HOUSE

My house is a haven for animals,
I suppose you could call it a zoo.
There's a bear in the chair drinking coffee,
And a mouse on the floor eating toffee.

Be careful where you stand when you wander around,
There might be the odd bone or dog that's lost it's home.
But don't be scared when you meet the rats,
They only want to sit on your lap.

I'd like to ask you a question,
Would you like to join my collection?
Of my brilliant zoo,
Hurry and give me an answer before my tiger swallows you up.

Lauren Walker (10)
Swain House Middle School

ALLITERATION

One wicked wizard wanted whales,
Two typhoons terrorise two towns,
Three Toms too tiny to go on the tornado,
Four fishing frogs frightened the fish,
Five frankfurters full of fries,
Six slimy sausages sizzled in the sun,
Seven surfing seals surrounded by sharks,
Eight elderly Eskimos entertained elephants,
Nine naughty Nigels nicked Nathan's Nike necklace,
Ten turtles tried on Taylor's trainers,
Eleven eels eating eggs,
Twelve ties tied to Timothy,
Thirteen telephones tangled to tissues,
Fourteen flies flying to France
Fifteen fierce foxes fought for food,
Sixteen ships sank slowly in the sea,
Seventeen songs sounded so sad,
Eighteen eagles eating empires,
Nineteen Nicky's all nearly nine,
Twenty teeth taking taxis.

Lee Storey (10)
Swain House Middle School

EASTER

Easter time is coming,
The resurrection of Jesus,
The boulder moving from the entrance.
The Easter Bunny is coming,
Delivering lots of chocolate eggs,
Hot cross buns symbolise the cross,
The eggs symbolise new life.
Some people get toys, some get chocolate.
Springtime is coming,
Chicks, bunnies and lambs being born,
Easter is a lunar festival,
There is no set date,
Usually it's March or April,
Pancake Day and Good Friday are all part of Easter.

Andrew Markham (11)
Swain House Middle School

MILLENNIUM

The year 2000 is almost here,
The Millennium Dome may be ready on time,
And inside the building aliens may arrive . . .
Deciding to take over Britain!
Computers will crash,
And cash will go flash . . .
Children will still go to school,
But have less days there!
That would be great - for the teachers as well,
Of course.
Excitement is growing
With all of the new things happening!
The only down side to it is that . . .
People have to pay more money to get to places.
Parties and celebrations will take place,
In the new year, century, *millennium*
So I will see you there!

Jessica McDonald (11)
Swain House Middle School

MILLENNIUM

Miraculous excitement is building up,
I can't wait until the millennium.
Late at night the clocks go twelve,
Leaping in excitement,
Everyone cheers,
Now we're in the millennium.
Nothing's changed,
I'm a bit disappointed,
Until now I've been excited.
Millennium has been and gone so fast!

Sarah Lyons (10)
Swain House Middle School

FOX HUNT

Over the hills the fox pounds,
Running away from the blood-thirsty hounds.
The huntsmen sound their horns,
As the fox dashes through a bed of thorns.

It struggles to run faster, tripping over its heels,
A pain in its chest the fox feels.
The horses parade on like a stampede.
Pounding through the brambles the fox starts to bleed.

As its heart beats faster the fox starts to slow down,
Trying to keep its paws on the ground.
The hunt is now quite a distance away,
Still chasing after its wanted prey.

'Tally-ho' the huntsman cried,
The fox lying on the ground with a gash in its side,
It tries hard to get to its feet,
But it loses hope of escaping the fleet.

It lies on the ground - its heart beating fast,
Another minute it will not last.
As the hounds approach it lets out a yelp -
Its last cry for help.

Stephanie Crawshaw (10)
Swain House Middle School

RAIN

Rain can be fast,
Rain can be slow,
Rain can flow in the wild wind blow.

Rain can trickle down icy windows,
Or,
Gush past streams of tiny creatures.

Rain can tremendously pour,
Or,
Drizzle in fair drops.

Drip . . . Drop . . .
The rain calms down,
And,
Freezes into a sparkling icicle,
As the warm, windy night cools.
Frost comes out.

Cherelle Christie (11)
Swain House Middle School

YEAR 2000

The year 2000 is sure to be,
Amazing and wonderful to see.
Some people said the world's going to end,
While others just drink and go round the bend.
Millennium Dome is on its way,
Then others just stare not knowing what to say.

The council are saying it will be ready,
The gasping guests are saying do be steady.
The computer bug is going round,
Computers are crashing without sound.
The millennium is nearly here,
Everybody give a *cheer!*

Sharanjit Kaur (11)
Swain House Middle School

SPACE AGE

We're approaching the year 2000,
What is also known as the space age.
Time rocket cars,
All flying in a rage.

Living on the moon,
Or in the middle of a sea.
A whole new future ahead,
I wonder what it holds for me.

I could become a pilot,
Of a dazzling spaceship.
I could become the second Einstein,
Or just serve fish and chips.

Someone could invent a time machine,
To take them back to the past.
They could come here to the present soon,
I hope they come fast.

What a wonder it would be,
If only my dream came true.
Unless an alien should eat me,
Oh, what should I do?

Christopher Chapman (11)
Swain House Middle School

SUBJECTS

History can be a bore,
Learning about the World War,
And PE can leave you sore.

English is absolutely great,
RE is what I hate,
I would just chat to a mate.

Maths and science are two of the main subjects,
Geography can be a pain,
Learning about Africa and Spain.

Katie Robertshaw (11)
Swain House Middle School

THIRTEEN LINES OF MAYHEM!

One wicked woman watched a weasel wickedly,
Two talking tortoises talked tonguelessly,
Three thumbs thought thoughtlessly,
Four faulty firemen fired fishermen,
Five fierce fish were fond of fishfingers,
Six stupid swans swam sleeplessly,
Seven singing sausages stopped, silently,
Eight enthusiastic eagles eating eggs on enormous elephants,
Nine naughty nuggets named nasty and nervous nuts in Nepal,
Ten tiny tigers told too many tongue-twisters in Tunisia, Tonga
and Thailand,
Navraj nearly nicked knickers and nails in Nuneaton,
Chas created chocolate in cold Cornwall,
Fred fried filthy flan on Fridays for funny falcons.

Manpreet Pooni (10)
Swain House Middle School

ONE HUNDRED AND TWENTY FRIENDS

One Willy Wally walked with William Whale,
Two Tilly Toms talked to the toilet,
Three Theodores thought thickly,
Four ferocious Francescas fiddled,
Five fabulous Fred's fingers fell off,
Six senseless Sams sighed,
Seven selfish Samanthas sucked sardines,
Eight Emilys annoyed everybody,
Nine naughty Nigels nipped Norman's knee,
Ten tanned Toms teeth tinged,
Eleven anonymous elephants ate eggs,
Twelve twits twiddled with twigs,
Thirteen thin theatres thought thoughtfully,
Fourteen foam foolish forks forever,
Fifteen funky fairies flew for food.

Claire Gordon (11)
Swain House Middle School

ALLITERATION

Alan the alligator ate apricots all awfully automatically in Angola,
Silly Sophie smelled stupid Sam's spoon,
Granny giggles, giggled, gigglefully, gloriously good,
Simon stored sweet sizzling sweets on stars.
Enormous Elizabeth emptied extra eggs to Emily,
Stupid Sarah slipped on some sloppy soup,
Andrew ate apples after August in Africa,
Nine naughty nits knitted nice noses,
Ten tatty Toms trotted to the toilet,
Eleven Erics eating enormous elephants in England,
Twelve Tims tidied tom's toys,
Joyful John jogged to Germany,
Suspicious Simon scribbled swiftly,
Fifteen ferocious families found food.

Bapinder Rana (10)
Swain House Middle School

LONELINESS

I am a lonely boy,
I sit in the corner of the playground,
Without a friend in the world,
Except for a little blackbird.

I see the seasons, wet and dry,
I see the months and years fly by.
I see it rain, I see it snow,
I see the children come and go.
I see them swinging fast and slow,
Upon the swing they love to go.

I see the gay expression near,
The reason why is very clear.
They have friends far and near,
Friends that walk and talk and hear,
I wish that I were like them,
Then I would never be sad again.

But what is this I start to hear?
There it is again, a tear.
I look around, and look again,
And then I see sat under a tree,
A little boy just like me.

I thought and thought and thought again,
And then . . . eureka, we could both be friends.
And after that we both were friends,
And friends we shall be to the end of the end.

Phillip Corner (11)
Swain House Middle School

THE MEDIEVAL WAR

Gallant knights and trusty foot soldiers,
Charge to war with lances and spears,
The enemy is a clever foe.
Shooting warriors with a well-targeted arrow.

Both sides clash,
With swords and daggers,
And blood patters and skin cut to tatters.

The knights charge in,
From the flanks of the army,
But with enemy sorcerers there,
That must be barmy!

The battle rages on and on,
And neither side will surrender,
No matter what.

At last the knights win,
As the king of the archers,
Moves no more.

Christopher Kalko (10)
Swain House Middle School

WHEN I WAS LITTLE

When I was little I used to play,
Aeroplanes, cats, shooting games,
And I built houses out of Lego.

I played with teddies, my favourite one was Berty.
I also played with action men and even had imaginary friends,
Like figures and army men.

With Lego and Duplo I made houses and buildings,
Such as mills, flats and even shops.

I helped my mum bake cakes, buns,
Biscuits and different goods.
I had lots of fun.

My favourite team is Leeds,
And my favourite car is a Ford Mondeo racing car.
I took it everywhere,
And I still remember it all now.

Joe Wade (11)
Swain House Middle School

WHEN I WAS LITTLE

When I was five I played with these toys,
Tracey Island, Lego and action boys.
We played on the mountain, we played in my den,
Before I kicked out my toy hen.
We fought and we fought up on the hill,
Before I got a toy till.

When I was six I played with this toy,
A red Action Man car that I pushed very far,
Up on the hills and far away where the other toys came to play.
There was Woody and Buzz and the rest of their friends,
Who were playing over the fence.

When I was seven I played in heaven with a teddy,
We played on the mountain, we played in the sea,
He went everywhere with me.

When I was eight I played with a car,
I drove up the hill and round the bend,
Before I had to stop and mend,
When it broke a tear in my eye,
And then after a little cry.

Scott Kirby (11)
Swain House Middle School

Tongue Twisting Alliteration

Rusting Rachel rioted round the roundabout,
Crazy Katie commented about Chloe's clothes,
Lots of lazy Lisa's lying in the lodge,
Sly Sidhra smiled on a ship to Spain,
Sarah sued Sainsburys for soggy sandwiches.

One weak woman wobbled to the west,
Two taunting twins teased two tired teachers,
Three theatrical thimbles thinking thoughtfully,
Four flying fish flipped on Friday,
Five fishermen fished frantically in France,
Six storming stubby stools stamped to San Francisco,
Seven stupid seals on safari,
Eight educated elephants enjoyed eating eggs.
Nine neglected nuns kneed Norma Nickley,
Ten test tubes tickled two text books.

Zoe Conroy (11)
Swain House Middle School

ALLITERATIVE ACES

One Willy Wonker walking round the world,
Two tickled tigers tortured tortoises,
Three thick thugs thought thoughtful thoughts,
Four fabulous fish phoned fishy friends,
Five folks fell for fool's gold,
Six slithery snakes slithered through seas,
Seven silly sailors sailed the seven seas,
Eight elephants ended everything.
Nine naughty nags never nagged nobody,
Ten torrid tigers tackled turtles,
Eleven electric eels electrocuted everyone,
Twelve tired teachers taught ten tables technology,
Thirteen thick thoughtful thickos thought thoughtful thicko thoughts,
Fourteen football fans fought Forest fans to figs,
Fifteen friends fought for freedom.

Ranvir Kalare (10)
Swain House Middle School

MY FOOTBALL POEM

My name is Saul. I play for Manchester United,
When they play I always get excited.
When I score a goal,
Everyone goes 'Yo!'

All referees in black,
When they give free kicks,
We all clap.
My mum and dad watch me,
And everyone goes potty.

I liked to play in the snow,
I don't like playing in the rain though.
I scored past Peter Schmeichel,
And I have a big smile.

Now that is my football poem,
Please keep on supporting,
I play tomorrow at noon,
And I hope to see you soon.

Carl Lomax (11)
Swain House Middle School

BLOCK ANGELES

What can you build with blocks?
Castles, houses, boats and docks.
There is so much more you can build with blocks.

Palaces with towers that are ever so high,
If you stand on them you can touch the sky.

I play with my blocks all the time,
I build and play in the sunshine.

From child to adult they are useful things,
Don't bother stopping when the telephone rings.

All the ships are returning to the docks,
All this you can build with blocks.

Ashley Perkins (11)
Swain House Middle School

ALLITERATION

One obvious ox obtaining oddments,
Two tacky tabbies taking tablets,
Three thoughtful tourists,
Four fantastic ferrets foraging for food,
Five fabulous functioning forms from far away,
Six scrumptious sausages sitting on a stool,
Seven small staring sheep,
Eight electric eels eating everything,
Nine numerous numbers never known,
Ten tasty trims of tripe,
Eleven elephants evacuating everywhere,
Twelve tortoises tasting tarts,
Thirteen thick thieves thinking thoughts,
Fourteen fighters fought for freedom,
Fifteen footballers fussed for a foul,
Sixteen singers shouting songs,
Seventeen squirrels squabbling for a scrumptious nut,
Eighteen enzymes eating everything,
Nineteen nannies nattering and nagging,
Twenty tigers trying to terrorise tourists.

Michael Pietkiewicz (11)
Swain House Middle School

BATHTIME

I pour in my last bit of bubblebath,
It foams up. Now I can start my adventure.

Sharky, Killer, Crocky too.
Nearly bathtime, they form a queue.
Squid, Ray and Polar Bear,
They all crowd round to get in there.

Turtle, Swordy, Little Bear,
Find their place upon the stair,
Dolphin, Whale and Octopus,
Push in line and make a fuss.

'It's time to get in' says Little Bear,
'Hurry up, Marshall's there.'
Hope it's foamy, hope it's warm,
It might be icy, there might be a storm.

'I'm diving in' says the Pelican,
'It's far too hot' shouts the old Toucan.
Come on everyone, follow me,
There's a whirlpool - there, you see.

Oh no, I've just found out,
It's nearly time for us all to get out,
Quickly swim and hide,
We can't, it's too strong a tide.

I love my bathtime in every way,
Except on Sunday, I must say.
It's just not fair, all my animals
Don't have to wash their hair.

Marshall Davies (10)
Swain House Middle School

MILLENNIUM

The Dome is finished!
Hip hip hooray!
That means the year 2000,
Is on its way.

New Zealand are the first to see,
The new millennium,
That is the key.

We'll walk on Mars,
There may be life,
We'll have a new date,
That would be nice.

What will it bring?
Nobody knows,
Could it bring happiness,
Or will it bring . . .
The world to a close!

Helen Wolstenholme (10)
Swain House Middle School

MY FAVOURITE TOYS

When I was a baby, my favourite teddy bear,
Was very small and very cute with lots of orange hair.
I used to coo and gurgle and hold my hands up too,
My mum and dad decided to call him Mr Who.

My Tiny Tears doll I loved so much,
Wherever I went this doll I'd clutch,
Her name was Lucy, she wore a pink dress,
Her hair was blonde and always a mess.

I liked playing with my friends,
Riding bikes and building dens,
Singing and dancing to different tunes,
Playing tea parties with cups and spoons.

Playing with Barbies was number one,
Messing about and having lots of fun.
High-heeled shoes and fashion design,
Whatever she wore the choice was mine.

Dolls and teddies are part of my past,
Playing time is going so fast.
Computer games and PC's too,
Now things of the future for me to view.

Ainsley Rhodes (11)
Swain House Middle School

MY WORLD

In a land far away,
The toys came alive today.
Sergeant Thunderbird at duty on base on Tracey Island,
Keeping watch for the baddies.
Buzz Lightyear sorts out his army for a day's work.
Out of nowhere came a deafening *Bang!*
'Pirates ahoy' Sergeant Thunderbird sang.
Then squeaking of rusty wheels,
Of cannons in place.
Now it's too late for Sergeant Thunderbird,
Boom!
The pirates hit his base.
Buzz commanded 'Fire at will.'
But he realised they were upon him,
This gave him a chill.
They fire at the pirates,
The pirates fire back.
'Oh no' both cannons blow each other's men far away.
Now my world has gone, it was all a dream,
But I will always remember,
My town by the sea.

Darren Brook (11)
Swain House Middle School

EVACUEES

Away today, away today,
I'm going away today.
No more sleeping in my bed,
No bombs to make me dead,
Mummy can't come nor can daddy,
Mustn't cry, must be happy.

Packed my case, packed my teddy,
Gas mask always at the ready,
All the children on the train,
Bye-bye London, bye-bye siren,
Slowly leave behind the city,
To the countryside, oh so pretty.

Hello lady, smile so sweetly,
I'll always be polite and elegant,
Please take me to your lovely home,
Keep me safe, I'll never roam,
I know I will always miss mummy,
Especially her good night kiss.

Hitler made the war so long,
I don't remember another home,
A real mother and a father,
A distant memory from afar,
So here I stay, safe and sound,
A brand new family all around.

Michelle Bell (11)
Swain House Middle School

ON THE STEAM TRAIN TO SAFETY

From the busy cities to the calm countryside,
What a lot of stress it must have been,
Travelling on the steam train,
With their gas masks over their shoulders,
Their lunches in one hand,
Then waving to their families,
Taken to places where they had not been,
Some sighs and cries, but to some it was an adventure,
Then getting chosen by their new families,
Then taken home to safety.

Daniel Wilson (11)
Swain House Middle School

EVACUEES

The children in the war,
Were sent away for sure,
To stop them being in danger,
They were sent to live with a stranger,
Some were happy, some were sad,
Some missed their mums, some missed their dads,
They went to the countryside with gas masks and clothes,
It was a frightening adventure, everybody knows,
In the middle of nowhere surrounded by trees,
They were called the evacuees.

Dawn Baker (11)
Swain House Middle School

WE WILL BE BACK

The Second World War had started,
Prime Minister Chamberlain announced,
We didn't know what would happen.
Maybe they would bomb our house.

We were taken to school as normal,
With packed lunch, gas mask and clothes.
We were going to the country,
But to where nobody knows.

They told us it would be safer,
Away from the terrors of war,
A lot of us were crying,
As we came out of the door.

We were having to leave our parents,
And afraid what would happen to them,
They told us not to worry,
And that we would soon be home again.

Ben Gray (10)
Swain House Middle School

TO THE COUNTRYSIDE

Evacuees, evacuees,
To the countryside we must flee,
Away from cities, away from towns,
In case the bombs come falling down.

I've left my mum,
I've left my dad,
And just right now,
I'm feeling sad.

The steam rises to the sky,
As we watch the fields go by.
The train trundles along,
And we all sing a song.

On the platform we all stand,
A stranger came to shake my hand,
I collect my things,
This is where my new life begins.

Greg Weston (10)
Swain House Middle School

THE OWL AND THE PUSSY CAT

The pussy cat asked the pig,
Please may I borrow your wig.
The pig agreed,
So they decided to go for a walk that day
To the woods where the bong trees grow.
It started to rain, thunder and hail,
The ground became difficult and soft,
And they became stuck in the mud,
The mud,
The mud,
And they became stuck in the mud.

Sarabdeep Olak (10)
Swain House Middle School

THE SEA

The sea is as deep as the ocean,
The sea looks like a whale's teeth,
When crashing on the shore,
It crumbles, rocks and kills the sand.

The sea can make noises like no one man,
It can kill when cold, it can kill when warm,
Below the surface is the unknown world,
Lurking down there are mysteries.

Rebecca Littlefair (11)
Woodhouse Grove School

OWL

As dark night falls he waits in silence,
For a mouse is a mouthful for a bird so cold.
As his wise eyes search and see
A scurrying along the ground,
He takes a graceful swoop and grabs his midnight feast.

Richard Hardman (11)
Woodhouse Grove School

THE SEA AND ME

The sea is calm and also rough,
It doesn't bother me because I'm tough.
The sea is like a roaring lion,
When it's calm, it's as flat as an iron.

The sand and sea go really well with me,
And that is why I go to sea,
The sun is really blazing, there I lie,
On the beach, lazing.

Sam Booth (11)
Woodhouse Grove School

SNAKE

The slithery snake waits,
Watches carefully and curiously,
The snake slithers silently through the grass.

Still watching,
Quietly slithering,
And then gets it.

William Myers (11)
Woodhouse Grove School

THE WILD CAT

In the dark woods,
The wild cat is stooped,
Waiting to pounce on his prey,
Silence is broke sharply by a rat with small footsteps,
He crunches on a large leaf,
The cat leaps on his scared prey.

Patrick Guilfoyle (12)
Woodhouse Grove School

THE SEA LIFE

The sea is like the collapsed sky,
The sea whispers as it rushes rapidly,
The sea charges as fast as a cheetah,
It is clean, clear and very salty.

The sea is as dangerous as a loose, wild tiger,
It is fast and the waves dash up and down,
The sea is like the melted moon,
To the sea animals, it is a home.

Hamza Darr (12)
Woodhouse Grove School

THE SEA

The sea is a big tank of water,
It also is an ocean of sea creatures,
Swimming round and round,
With miles of seaweed for sea creatures to eat,
From miles around.

The sea is also physically fearful,
The sea is salty and strong,
It crushes your bones like a digesting stomach,
And keeps you lying at the bottom for ever.

Harriet Couch (11)
Woodhouse Grove School

THE OWL

Perched in the cold quiet of the mill,
She watches the spill.

In the corner there's a stir,
A sound which warns her.

From above the abandoned stall,
She starts her murderous fall.

John Lindsey (12)
Woodhouse Grove School

THE OWL

In the wild, wet, windy night,
The owl precariously perches in the tree,
Wondering what tasty treat he'll feast upon
Tonight.

Focusing on the defenceless, weak creature,
He silently swoops upon his prey,
Darting and diving like a bolt of
Lightning.

Rachel Oxtoby (12)
Woodhouse Grove School

THE EVER-CHANGING SEA

The sea can be like a summer's sky,
But can turn into a raging storm.
It can break bones like a dropping brick,
But can then be a necklace, sparkling on someone's neck.

It can bring tidal waves as high as the moon,
It can suck you down, deeper and deeper.
It can be a relaxing place, where you can swim or splash about:
It's the ever-changing sea!

Paul Genders (11)
Woodhouse Grove School

THE WOLF

Below the moon, behind the trees,
The wolf is watching, waiting, wanting.
He hears a sound then sees a mouse,
He quietly grins getting ready to pounce.
Then like an arrow he pounces, fast,
He eats his fill and howls at long last.

Louise Girling (12)
Woodhouse Grove School

THE SEA LIFE

The sea is cool,
Crystal blue and sparkly.
It's the home for many creatures,
It is colourful and crisp.

The sea is like a bulldozer,
It destroys and clears,
The sea is an athlete,
Strong and fast.

Daniel Drimer (11)
Woodhouse Grove School

THE SEA'S MOODS

The sea is like a velvet sheet,
Spread across the floor.
It crashes against crooked cliffs,
Erasing them even more.
The sea is fire,
Unpredictable, unsure,
Creeping steadily across land,
Until the shore is unseen.

Natalie Gaines (12)
Woodhouse Grove School

WOLF

Waiting in glistening moonlight,
His spiky spines arise,
Surrounded by gleaming stars.

The wind waves,
As the moaning trees sway,
Gone, gone, gone as the whistling wind.

Jan Ali (12)
Woodhouse Grove School

THE BEAR

He hides behind a mouldy oak tree,
Claws as long as a gigantic bee,
Waiting to pounce for his tea.

Waiting, waiting for the right moment,
One wrong move could blow his cover,
Jumps, then kills this tasty treat.

Oliver Szymanski (12)
Woodhouse Grove School

THE OWL

The big owl lurked in the black wood,
Watching a small black shadow,
Its talons piercing the large oak tree,
His bright eyes surveying the ground,
The black shadow ran for its life,
As the big owl swooped down.

Sam Pearson (12)
Woodhouse Grove School

THE CHEETAH

In the dark night it is easier for him,
In the green grass he prowls,
Slowly he moves while he waits for his prey,
Hoping it's abandoned.
He hungrily sees his coming feast,
He moves slowly towards it and then the speedy chase is on,
With a loud thud he goes down - boom!

Frederick Wallace (12)
Woodhouse Grove School